Making My Breakfast

Learning the Sequential Steps of a Process

Judi Austin

Rosen Classroom Books & Materials
New York

Every morning I go to the kitchen to make my breakfast.

First I find a glass, a spoon, and a bowl.
I put them on the table.

I fill the glass with orange juice.

Then I drink the juice.

Next I put some cereal in the bowl.

Then I add milk to the cereal.

I use my spoon to eat the cereal
and milk.

I take my glass, spoon, and bowl to the kitchen sink.

I wash everything carefully.

I put the glass, spoon, and bowl in the rack to dry.

Now I am finished with my breakfast!

Words to Know

bowl

cereal

glass

kitchen

orange juice